MICHIGAN HAUNTS
PUBLIC PLACES, EERIE SPACES

MICHIGAN HAUNTS
PUBLIC PLACES, EERIE SPACES

Jon Milan and Gail Offen
Foreword by Rev. Gerald S. Hunter

ARCADIA
PUBLISHING

Published by Arcadia Publishing
Charleston, South Carolina

Printed in the United States of America

Library of Congress Control Number: 2019940830

For all general information, please contact Arcadia Publishing:
Telephone 843-853-2070
Fax 843-853-0044
E-mail sales@arcadiapublishing.com
For customer service and orders:
Toll-Free 1-888-313-2665

Visit us on the Internet at www.arcadiapublishing.com

CONTENTS

FOREWORD

This book invites you to take a road trip. A very unusual road trip, to visit seemingly ordinary public venues and businesses—the types of places we often drive past without giving a second thought. Then, this book encourages you to take a second look because these places are "extra" ordinary. They are all haunted.

As far back as I can remember, I have been interested in things that go bump in the night. You know what I mean—ghosts and apparitions (yes, there is a difference between the two), the unexplained movement of inanimate objects, the sounds of voices and music when there's nary a physical soul around to produce either.

I have been asked many times why I have been so interested in such things. The answer is simple: way back in 1965, when I was 12 years old, our family moved into a haunted farmhouse—a very haunted farmhouse.

No imagination was needed when it came to entertainment, as that was provided for us whether we desired it or not. Unseen hands often opened or closed our bedroom doors, just as invisible feet would often tread heavily across the creaky old flooring. More than once, one of us would glance into a dresser mirror and discover our reflection was not the only one looking back at us. And it was not all that unusual to walk into the kitchen or the living room and find yourself in the presence of an uninvited guest who, considering their sense of fashionable attire, had long ago made their exit from the physical world.

Having spent the formative years of my youth living among those various and active ghosts, I developed a deep desire to understand all things paranormal. My undergraduate work at Albion College included instruction in Jungian psychology, the power of myth, and the interpretation of dreams. My graduate work at the Methodist Theological School in Ohio is where I explored the religious dimensions of life after life.

When I began my work in this discipline over 40 years ago, there were not many of us who shared a desire to understand why some people and places are haunted while others are not. I have visited hundreds of haunted dwellings, interviewed thousands of people who have had ghostly encounters, written three books about hauntings in Michigan, lectured widely, and been the subject of newspaper articles and television segments.

I recommend this book because it includes only those places I am convinced are truly haunted. In fact, I have been acquainted with virtually all of them.

These days, dozens upon dozens of books are available that deal with supposedly "haunted" places. I cast a jaundiced eye upon many of the "paranormal investigation teams" that seem to have permeated our society. Too many of them may possess the latest expensive ghost hunting gadgets yet still enter into a private dwelling or a public setting all too ready to declare proof the places harbor the spirits of the dead. I am far too skeptical of their approach. After all, not every speck of dust is a ghostly "orb," and every chilly corner is certainly not necessarily indicative of the dead sucking the heat out of a room.

So, take the road trips at your leisure, but remember that just because you may be eager to talk about the ghosts, those who own or work in the places you visit may not be. Be polite and respectful. Simply make mention that you have heard the place may be haunted. If, for whatever reason, they do not want to talk about it, honor that. And remember, ghosts are just people who continue to hang around for reasons of their own. Just as the living avoid rude people, so do the dead.

Now, get started. Buy and read this book. Then grab your camera, gas up the car, and head out on a ghostly adventure all your own.

—Rev. Gerald S. Hunter, 2019

ACKNOWLEDGMENTS

This book was made possible through the efforts, assistance, generosity, patience, and support of many. We would like to thank Cloryssa Ackerman, Brenda Baker, Chris Behler, Brighton Chamber of Commerce, Robert C. Brown, Scott Burns, Cassey Case, Mason Christensen, Samantha Christman-Ailes, the Detroit Institute of Arts (DIA), Tyler DePerro, Robert DeVos, Ron DeVos, Sarah Dowdell, Kelly Felder, Sharon Fisher, Karrie Green, Leslie Gregory, Sherri Gregory, James Berton Harris, Jessica Herczeg-Konecny, Liliani Ho, Jennifer Isbister, Danni LaDuke, Wayne Martinez, Pamela McConeghy, Dorrie Milan, Cynthia Motzenbecker, Kirstyn Mularski, John Polzin, Tracy Ritter, Kylie Ruettinger, Tim Ruff, Stanley S., Christine Schinker, Rudy Simons, Alexander Smith, Dianna Stampfler, Chris Stone, Craig Tascius, Steve Thrall, David V. Tinder (posthumous), Robert Vedro, John and Sandy Vyletel, Jon Wasko, Dave West, Joe Zainea, and Duane Zemper (posthumous). And, as always, Randy Samuels, "Here's to you!"

And special thanks go to Rev. Gerald S. Hunter, Keith M. Steffke, and the Steffke Memorial Maritime Collection (SMMC).

Unless otherwise indicated, all images featured in this book are from the collection of the authors.

Images noted as courtesy of the David V. Tinder Collection are courtesy of the David V. Tinder Collection of Michigan Photography, Clements Library, University of Michigan.

Images noted as courtesy of Keith Steffke are courtesy of Keith M. Steffke and the SMMC.

INTRODUCTION

About 20 years ago, I owned a 1928 two-story duplex in Dearborn. My lifelong friend and bandmate Rick Pinkerton (co-owner of the gone but legendary Music Menu in Greektown) became my second-floor tenant. One evening, shortly after we moved in, Rick came downstairs and said, "Y'know, Milan, I think this house may be haunted!" He was a true skeptic but described how, when getting up to use the bathroom, he felt as though something was trying to physically knock him down. I had actually heard the loud thuds. Stranger still, that morning he had awakened around 3:00 a.m. because he heard water pouring into the bathtub.

After that, I became aware of strange sounds coming from upstairs when Rick was at work—and we both heard odd noises and banging coming from the attic. After an animal control service determined nothing had ever been up in the attic, I called Gerald Hunter.

I had read his first Haunted Michigan book. Gerald's approach is to always start by looking for logical explanations. He is a great observer who has found many unexplained things. He is also an ordained Methodist minister. He immediately asked me to rule out several possibilities, including animals in the attic or something falling on the tub faucet handle. Nothing had.

When Rick was at work, it was never surprising to hear someone running back and forth upstairs or a crash coming from the living room. But when I would go up there—nothing!

Eventually, Rick moved out. The night he left, I was again awakened by the sound of running upstairs.

"Stop it!" I yelled, and it immediately stopped.

I just started laughing. I mean, how do you explain such a thing?

Once, I stopped at home during my lunch hour and heard the unmistakable sound of water running in the tub. I ran up to the unoccupied apartment and shut off the water—it took four complete turns. As soon as the water was off, I heard a chair scraping loudly in the living room and some excited whispering. I simply turned toward the living room and yelled, "Yeah, I know you're there!"

Another night, I was leaving home in a hurry when I realized I had not left a light on. When I pulled into my driveway about 10:30 that night, I was stunned to see every light in my house was on—on both floors and in the basement!

Later that spring, Brian Harris, who played drums in my band (he now owns Harris Conservatory of Music in Plymouth), wanted to pick up his drums. He was unaware of the strange goings-on at the house.

When he arrived at our gig, Brian handed me the key he borrowed and said, "Wow, your upstairs tenants must be a real piece of work! I was barely there 30 minutes, and they kept pounding on the floor."

"Ah," I said, with a slight nod. "I don't have a tenant."

Brian looked at me and laughed nervously, "Well, there was definitely someone upstairs."

"Yeah, I know," I said, "but I have no idea who it is."

Brian gave me a look.

"You get used to it," I replied. And somehow, I did.

Eventually, I sold the house. But it left me with a fascination about other places with haunted stories. There are so many spots in Michigan with legends, sightings, sounds, and unexplained activity. But since you cannot visit private homes, my coauthor and I decided to focus on public places. We hope you will visit these locations and draw your own conclusions. And, if nothing else, you will see a lot of our fascinating state.

—Jon Milan

One

RESTAURANTS AND
WATERING HOLES

VORGESCHMACK. Visiting a haunted restaurant or tavern is the perfect aperitif for thirsty, time-crunched paranormal adventurers, and Brooklyn's Cherry Creek Winery is ripe for an initial tasting. Built in 1870, this old schoolhouse is where wine tasters attend class by the glass. And though school's out forever, one ghostly little girl is still in attendance—a bit shy, she is often seen peeking out from the back room. More wine?

WHATCHU TALKIN 'BOUT, WILLIS? The tiny village of Willis is best-known for Bone Heads BBQ, where some customers never seem to leave. Housed in a structure dating from 1865, Bonehead's has several paranormal patrons—including a window washer from the "otherworld employment agency"—frequently seen from the street. There is also Nellie, often seen descending the stairs in a white dress, and a little girl who sometimes appears in the mirror of the women's bathroom.

WALTZ OPUS POSTHUMOUS. The Waltz Inn began as a biergarten in the 19th century, long before becoming the popular and haunted eatery it is today. A previous owner named Tom is thought to be "haunter-in-chief," and his silent apparition has been spotted sitting on an upstairs couch, staring out windows and standing in the kitchen. He is a prankster and has been known to turn lights on late at night and slam the freezer door.

Hotel New Hudson, Mich

So, This Ghost Walks into a Bar . . . A stagecoach stop known as the Old Tavern along the old Grand River Trail between Detroit and Lansing, the New Hudson Inn looks pretty much unchanged since 1831. In fact, it is now the oldest continuously operating bar in Michigan. During a recent renovation, a hidden room that the New Hudson historical society believes was used for hiding fugitive slaves along the Underground Railroad was discovered (at right). The opening exposed in the ceiling would have been concealed within a hollow, wooden support pillar extending to the floor, with a ladder inside to the secret room. With so many well-kept secrets, there is no telling how who might have come and gone here—and some who never left. Perhaps that explains some of the seldom-seen tenants who make their presence known on an almost daily basis.

WEEKLY AND ETERNAL RATES AVAILABLE. With so much history, the inn is bound to have a few customers who have been around for a while. Although no longer a hotel, the New Hudson's workmen have made eye contact with more than a few disappearing residents upstairs, including one wearing a Civil War–era uniform. They have also harvested some unusual things concealed within the walls (above). And, of course, there are the ghostly patrons known to hang out late at the bar, only to disappear when approached. Waitress Karrie says hardly a day goes by without some strange occurrence: "Sometimes the girls are grabbed by unseen hands or someone brushes by, and no one's there." There is even a rude, unshaven male spirit who was seen in the ladies' room. Although motorcycles have replaced stagecoaches, travelers still love to stop at the inn.

ROAD WORTHY. Hungry travelers—and ghosts—have stopped here since 1831, when Enoch Fifield welcomed stagecoaches on the route linking Jackson to northern Michigan. Across the street from a Native American burial ground, it became the Meadow Lark Inn in 1924, which doubled as a speakeasy during Prohibition. In fact, there is a tunnel in the basement where illegal liquor was stored—and a slain gangster is rumored to be buried. Called the Roadhouse since the late 1960s, odd legends abound. An old piano in the back sometimes plays by itself. Waitstaff report that they back into or are pushed by something when no one is there. Ghostly faces sometimes appear in the kitchen order window (below) or walk through the bar. Once, a spice rack flew off the wall, almost hitting a waiting entree. Apparently, the food needed more seasoning.

A Toast to Thomas. Howell's MainStreet Winery has its own ghost, but he is a little too young to drink: a seven-year-old child named Thomas. He hangs out in the back, running up and down the stairs, and occasionally moves wine bottles or turns radios on and off. This late-1800s building was formerly a saloon and a paint store, and perhaps the owners' kids just never left the back room.

Gandy Dancer. A slang term for a railroad worker, this 1886 Romanesque stone building in Ann Arbor was known as the finest station on the Michigan Central line between Buffalo and Chicago. Unclaimed bodies were kept in the basement during World War l, leading to reports of restless spirits. Chuck Muer made it a fine restaurant in 1970, complete with a discerning, well-dressed ghost that is sometimes seen in the halls.

SHIRO TERROR. Condensed milk heir Charles Rogers built Novi's White House Manor in 1929 and dreamed of seeing a daughter descend its grand staircase (at right) on her wedding day. Instead, he had sons, and the honor fell to a granddaughter; however, she opted for a "condensed" wedding and eloped. Devastated, Charles died that night. Years later, Charles's widow was laid in state in the library (were they going for the haunted Triple Crown?). Today, it is Shiro, a Japanese restaurant where guests enjoy dinner along with the occasional paranormal activity. These include standard disembodied voices, lights turning on and off, and doors opening and closing, upgraded with a side dish of silverware mysteriously returned to drawers (did the butler die here, too?) and shattered mirrors in the barroom (formerly the library). Hauntings are not available for carry out—one hopes.

"OLDEST DIVE BAR IN DETROIT." That is how Mary Aganowski describes the Two-Way Inn. It was also voted the number-one dive bar in the USA. Mary has been here since she was 17, when her father bought the historic bar dating from 1876. Soon after they moved in, Mary's mother spotted a bearded man sitting on her bed. Subsequent research identified him as the original owner, Col. Philetus W. Norris (left). Once she saw the photograph, her mother said, "That's him!" Then, things got even more interesting: "One morning, a barmaid was on the phone when a woman in a nightgown walked past to where the walk-in cooler is in back. When I came in a short time later, the barmaid said, 'You sure changed fast!' We spent an hour looking for her. We figured she spent the night here, but we never found her."

ACCORDING TO MARY (ABOVE). Mary Aganowski continues, "Eventually, we got used to the jukebox playing on its own or TVs going on and off, but the craziest thing is the ladies' room. Sometimes, when you try to enter, the door pushes back and slams shut. First time it happened, I figured someone was in there, but when I looked in, no one was there. It's happened a lot over the years, and we always tell the ladies no one's in there, but they insist there *has* to be, since someone pushed the door shut. But, it's always the same—no one's there. We think it's the colonel's daughter, Ida. He didn't die here, but she did. Sometimes people ask if I want to get rid of the spirits, and I always tell them, 'No, this is their place; I can live with 'em!' "

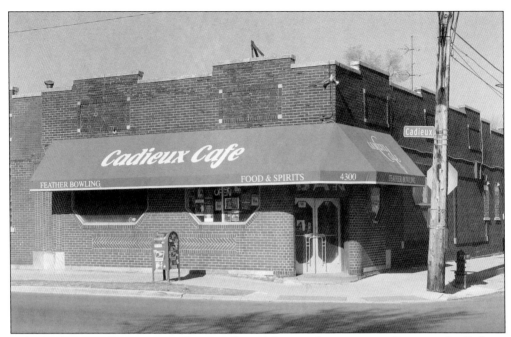

Mussels, Feather Bowling and Ghosts. One of the worst kept secrets in Detroit is the Cadieux Cafe. It has been a neighborhood hangout serving mussels and beer since Prohibition, when it had to be a secret. It has always been a hub of Flemish culture, which made it the perfect fit when Robert and Yvonne Devos (pictured below) bought it after leaving Belgium in 1962. Apparently, they liked it so much, they never left. Many people have caught a glimpse of the late Yvonne seated at her table next to the feather bowling alley, where she and son Ron (facing page) had coffee every morning. "I still sit there," Ron adds. "You can definitely sense her presence." Once, Ron called to speak to the manager, and Yvonne answered the phone. "I knew it was her—the voice and accent were unmistakable. Then, she was gone."

SPIRITED ENTERTAINMENT. One morning, a manager spotted Yvonne at her usual table. The apparition simply smiled and promptly disappeared. But several spirits are present at the Cadieux, including Ron's grandfather Alfred, who once identified himself with a ghostly hug. Manager Wayne Martinez recalls how, one late night, a woman emerged from the ladies' room. When he approached her, she dissipated into a flash of smoky vapor. Several years ago, a regular customer was killed crossing Cadieux Street. Now, many claim to see someone running toward them from the street then suddenly disappear. Ron tells how he once heard water running in the men's room. When he walked in, it was running full blast, and the water had reached the top of the basin. Suddenly, the faucet shut off by itself, and the water emptied down the drain.

Luna Si. In 1939, just after a brief lunch, 19-year-old stenographer Mina Decker returned to her office in the Judd Building on Ionia Street in Grand Rapids. There were few people in the building at that time of day, but one individual—who will forever remain unknown—was waiting for her and bludgeoned her to death with a hammer. The mystery was never solved, but the haunting began. Today, the Judd Building is home to Luna Taqueria, a popular restaurant known for tacos and creative cocktails. The employees playfully attribute "creative" brush-bys, unexpected "trick of the lights", and the occasional door opening and closing on its own as the work of "Henry," the name they have given the ghost—though it might be Mina, the murderer, or at least someone who knows who did it.

STRANGERS IN THE NIGHT. Jackson's Bella Notte restaurant is a local favorite with a cozy, intimate atmosphere—the main floor dining room is encircled by the balcony of a mezzanine dining area. There is also a ballroom. But, ask the staff about the "extra" help, and they might mention a few who are not on the payroll. Owner Annette Walker is happy to talk about them; she even has names for them. Some are playful, and others go about their business in an unusual manner, like the woman diners watched ascending an invisible stairway before disappearing into the wall. Employee Dave West tells of a man in white pants he often glimpses jumping out of sight when he goes into the basement. Gerald Hunter features the restaurant in *Haunted Michigan 3*, and it is fascinating reading.

FRISKY AND WHISKEY. Even if you dine alone at the Fenton Hotel, you will be surrounded by people—some of them more alive than others; however, the dead are pretty lively here. There is frequently a ghost at table 32 who orders a shot of whiskey and then disappears when it arrives. Or the "handsy" ghost who pinches the waitstaff's backsides. Perhaps one will run into the man wearing a top hat. Then, there is Emery, the former custodian who lived upstairs and considers this a job for life—or death. Owner Nick Sorise takes this all in stride. He has even taken a ghostly phone call himself. He once told an employee not to use the house phone for personal calls. As the employee walked away, the phone rang, and Nick picked it up. A scary, deep voice at the other end said, "No personal calls!"

UPSTAIRS, DOWNSTAIRS. Although the upper floors of this historic 1856 building are now used for storage, the staff is not crazy about going up there. They have seen everything from a bearded man, looking in from the outside, to Emery pacing his old room. So hang around the inviting dining room. The fish is recommended here, and if the reader happens to be at Fenton's table 32, do not forget to pay for the whiskey!

HUNGRY JACK. Allegan's Grill House is guaranteed to satisfy hunger and a taste for the paranormal. Built in 1836, it was once a popular watering hole for itinerant lumberjacks. In 1847, one was killed and buried on the premises—and he is still here. Known as Jack, he likes to materialize on occasion, as well as dim lights, rearrange furniture, change radio stations, and leave a shot of whiskey on the bar. (Courtesy of The Silo Banquets and Catering.)

A **REAL COLD CASE.** Somerset's Deck Down Under began as the Moonlight Chalet, a two-story tavern, in the 1920s. Later, the upstairs burned, and strange things began happening when a subsequent owner attempted renovation—five wall-mounted mirrors shattered at the same time. When Sue Brunty bought it, she renamed it Lakeside Lounge, but the mysteries continued. She shared many with Gerald Hunter for *Haunted Michigan,* including the time she and an employee finished stocking the cooler and then suddenly heard a woman's voice talking inside. "Shut up in there," the employee joked, and the voice stopped. When they opened the cooler, it was empty. The apparition of a woman has been seen here often, and old-timers recall the original owner's violent relationship with his wife and how, one day, she mysteriously disappeared, never to be heard from again.

Two

Asylums, Sanitariums, Orphanages, Schools, Hospitals, and Prison

INDELIBLE IMAGES. Places considered haunted are often associated with sorrow and suffering. Perhaps the incredible energy emitted through trauma creates the phenomenon known as place memory—the visual and audible imprint of things past. Above, the allegedly haunted silos of the abandoned Detroit House of Corrections (DeHoCo) work farm at Five Mile and Ridge Road, Plymouth. While the ruins are visible from the road, many areas are posted "No Trespassing."

FROM TB TO HEEBIE-JEEBIES. Howell's "San," as it was nicknamed, was Michigan's first tuberculosis sanatorium, built on the highest point in Southeast Michigan. It went from 16 beds when it was built in 1907 to 500 beds in 1930. Antibiotics eventually eliminated the threat of TB, so the San began accepting patients with mental disabilities. It closed in 1982, and many of the buildings and graveyard were demolished, replaced by an upscale subdivision. Of course, what is believed to be former patients still live—well, remain—there. Area residents have reported seeing spirits in hospital gowns wandering; one even has a rope around his neck. There have been many reports of paranormal activity in these houses. Although very dangerous, there are also tunnels that remain in the ruins of the San, which ghost hunters and others continue to explore.

WOMANS SHACK "WILSON," MICH. STATE SANATORIUM, HOWELL.

Willow Lake Asylum Grounds, Traverse City, Mich.

BEAUTY AS THERAPY. That was the intention when Dr. James Munson ran the Northern Michigan Asylum in Traverse City (aka Willow Lake State Hospital) starting in 1885. No restraints were used, there were lots of flowers, and every patient had a room with a lovely view. Over the years, it became everything from a TB Sanitorium to a drug rehab center. Now known as The Village, it houses shops and restaurants, such as the acclaimed Trattoria Stella. Yet, there are still sightings of roaming, hospital gown-clad patients, unexplained lights, and Electronic Voice Phenomena (EVP) in the building. A ghost of a priest that committed suicide shows up in the former chapel. Nearby are the "Hippie Trees"—remains of trees that were once considered gateways to hell but are now just colorful art. Take the Village's historic tours, which include walking the original tunnels.

Catholic Orphanage, Marquette, Mich.

HALLOWED GROUND. Holy Cross Orphanage in Marquette has a tragic past. This 1915 building is now apartments, but for years, it housed Native American children. There are mixed stories about their treatment by the nuns, but some persist, including a girl who died after being punished and left outside in the winter. While it was abandoned, many visitors heard sobbing children's voices as well as sounds of play.

Warriner Hall, Central Mich. College Mt. Pleasant, Mich.

AFTER-SCHOOL ACTIVITIES. Warriner Hall at Central Michigan University is said to be haunted by 19-year-old Theresa Schumacher, who was killed by a descending elevator after putting her head through a small window in the third-floor elevator door in 1937. Since then, phantom footsteps and loud knocking have been heard throughout the building, and several students have reported seeing Theresa's ghost on the fifth floor.

Gov Indian School' Mt. Pleasant' Mich.   16/62

NOT PLEASANT. Built in 1892 to educate Native American children, the Mount Pleasant Indian Industrial Boarding School has a sad past. The abusive staff tried to erase their language and customs. Hundreds of Native children are said to be buried there. The building was later used as a mental hospital and has been closed since 2010. Figures have been seen roaming the grounds, and there have been reports of moans, crying, and screams. Note that this is now the property of the Saginaw Chippewa Tribal Nation, who hope to make it a museum. Be respectful, do not trespass here, and be aware that it a patrolled area.

LOOKING ACROSS THE LAKE ELOISE MICH.

NOT DEAD, JUST FORGOTTEN. In London, it was Bedlam; in New York, Bellevue, and around Detroit, it was Eloise—where they took you when they were "coming to take you away." The Wayne County Poorhouse and Sanitarium began in Detroit as a multipurpose repository for undesirables, as well as a debtors' prison and asylum for the mentally unstable, drunkards, drug addicts, and the elderly who suffered from dementia. In 1839, it was relocated to the wilderness: a dwelling along the Old Chicago Road once known as the Black Horse Tavern. At the time, it had 35 patients or inmates, but by 1900 it had 10,000 housed in 75 buildings spread over 902 acres. It was a place of nightmares, with shock treatments and psychiatric experimentation. If one ever expects a place to be haunted, this is it.

POWER HOUSE ELOISE.
J.H. CAVE DETROIT

ELOISE, MICHIGAN. By 1894, it was renamed Eloise, for the daughter of a board executive, and registered as a Michigan city. It had its own post office, train station, farm, factories, and a fire department; many buildings were connected by a network of tunnels. Over time, thousands were sent there, never to be heard from again. The unclaimed dead were buried across the street, with graves—more than 7,000—marked only by numbered stones (right). Until it closed in 1984, it was common to see sad and hopeless patients endlessly rocking on wooden swings behind the tall iron fences and hear the intermittent wail of alarms whenever someone attempted to escape. After it closed, tales of haunting began: the ghostly apparition of a woman in white in windows and on rooftops, lights appearing in long-abandoned buildings, and the unearthly sound of growling near the children's playground.

THE HAUNTED GROCERY AND THE WOMAN IN BLACK. After many buildings were demolished, the county began selling the land where Eloise once stood. A grocery store and plaza emerged along the corner. Soon, employees began reporting apparitions of elderly men and women appearing in the store aisles, only to disappear moments later. Many employees referred to it as the haunted Kroger, and some avoided transferring there. In 2002, coauthor Milan was taking photographs behind the plaza and captured the above image. It was taken along a fenced area of the ruins, and the close-up (below) appears to reveal a woman in a long black dress wearing a hat. When the photograph was taken, no one was there, and when he returned, he found nothing along the fence that resembled the image. Eloise ruins are not open to the public, and trespassing is unlawful.

BUSY BODIES. Dr. Horace Mellus built the first hospital in Brighton in 1931. It has served over time as a church office, teen center, and even a chocolate shop. But it was its years as a hospital and morgue that dredge up ghostly tales. This chute (below) is where body parts were dumped and sent to the incinerator in the basement. A lot of paranormal activity has been documented down there, along with stories from people who worked in the building. On the second floor, in the former operating room, people have felt the presence of others, as well as pressure on their chests. It has a spooky past, but now the building is beautifully restored and the home of the Brighton Chamber of Commerce, with friendly (and live) spirits working there.

WATCH YOUR STEP. Sometimes, shadowy figures are seen roaming the grounds. Perhaps these are manifestations of former Mellus patients who never left. There are even rumors of body parts being buried way out back. This is the back morgue stairway—but one will probably want to use the front entrance.

HAUNTED HALL. In 1945, Dominican Sisters relocated Grand Rapids's Aquinas College to the estate of industrialist Edward Lowe. Built in 1909, it provided accommodations for Theodore Roosevelt. This central campus building became Holmdene Hall, but security and housekeeping staff thought Haunted described it better. With phantom elevator riders, disembodied children's voices, and apparitions disappearing into walls, it is little wonder why campus police initiate new recruits by having them make nightly rounds alone.

Three

HOTELS, INNS, B&BS, AND STAGECOACH STOPS

THE WALKER TAVERNS. Sixty-five miles west of Detroit lie the Irish Hills, a region of rolling hills and glacial lakes. For the Algonquian, it was a mystical place; for 19th-century travelers, it was a fearsome region. Considered haunted and rife with bandits, it was said that many who entered were never seen again. Those travelers willing to take a chance often found refuge for the night at the Walker Tavern. (David V. Tinder Collection.)

THE INCREDIBLE MR. HIPSLEY. Sylvester and Lucy Walker purchased the tavern in 1842. It still stands at the junction of US Route 12 and the Monroe Pike, where it provided lodging for many (including Daniel Webster and James Fenimore Cooper). However, at least one guest checked in and never checked out. Apparently, during the 1840s, a man named Hipsley, of Van Wert, Ohio, stopped in and, after an evening of drinking and cards, retired to his room. In the morning, he was gone, and all that remained was a large blood stain on the floor. His horse turned up days later, but Hipsley was never seen again. Perhaps he is the one haunting the tavern where EVP are often recorded, and airborne anomalies are seen and captured on film. One investigator asked, "Who was murdered here?" A recorded EVP replied, "Hipsley."

Two Haunted Taverns, No Waiting. In 1852, Walker built the Brick Walker Tavern (above), complete with a ballroom, directly across from the original tavern. Now a private business, the Brick Walker seems to be haunted by at least one of the party guests from a doomed New Year's party in 1863, when a winter storm sent revelers home early and one young woman to her grave. Just a mile down the road is the Junction of Person Highway. It was here, in front of the Siam School (at right) that a road crew unearthed the remains of nine Potawatomi in 1924 (later reinterred next to the Walker Tavern). On a farm nearby, the preserved body of a Potawatomi child was unearthed by farm workers in the 19th century; once exposed to the air, it fell to dust. The story, recounted years later by the farmer's wife in local papers, tells how a strange and silent Native American woman appeared at the door later that night, apparently to claim her lost child.

BEWARE OF THE BISCUITS. Most people driving by the stately Alhambra in Detroit (above) have no idea that it was the scene of a famous scandal at the turn of the century. Built in 1898, with Harvey Firestone as one of its tenants, the Alhambra employed a cook named Rose Barron who was demoted to a scrubwoman in 1905. She responded by putting arsenic in a batch of biscuits, poisoning 19 people, 2 of whom died. Rose's trial was sensational and well-covered in the tabloids. Her lawyer convinced the jury that the poisoning was the result of faulty plumbing, and Rose was acquitted. Not so coincidentally, perhaps, it was later discovered that her father-in-law also died of arsenic poisoning. Passers-by have seen faces in the upper windows of the long-abandoned building, as well as hearing moans.

CALL HIM "AL." Also known as the Pick Fort Shelby, this popular 1916 hotel added an Albert Kahn–designed 21-story tower in 1927. For years, it was a hangout for reporters from the two Detroit newspapers, whose offices were down the street. It closed for good in 1974. A one-eyed man named Al squatted in the basement of the abandoned hotel and ran errands for the nearby Anchor Bar. During the 1980s, the old hotel's plumbing gave out, and four feet of sewage flowed into the basement, drowning poor Al in what might be the ickiest crime scene ever (medical examiners said his bones were stripped clean) Al's ghost is said to haunt the alley behind the hotel as well as the lobby. He is probably happy knowing the Fort Shelby is now beautifully restored as the Doubletree Hotel—one of the first in Detroit's turnaround.

Vintage Ghosts. The Linden Hotel in Linden is the longest continuously operated business in Genesee County. A stagecoach stop in the 1840s, the Linden Hotel is now a restaurant and bar that is proud of its haunted history. A friendly ex-patron named Chuck haunts his old room. The waitstaff feels unexpected tugs when no badly mannered customer is around. Also, a ghostly Confederate soldier (a long way from home) shows up in photographs.

Oh, Fudge! One of America's most beautiful hotels, Mackinac Island's Grand may also be one of its most haunted. Built over an old burial ground, guests have reported odd events, such as hovering entities, top-hatted men, and little Rebecca, often seen floating down hallways. But during the wee hours, don't forget to check the front porch (the world's longest)—one might just see the ghostly "woman in black" walking her dog.

PURPLE MEETS GREEN. Clare takes its name from the beautiful county in Ireland—and the still-thriving Doherty Hotel takes its haunted fame from the Purple Gang. Built in 1924, the gang headed there when things heated up in Detroit. It was a speakeasy, with gambling and high-end prostitution. The hotel Tap Room bar (below) gained national attention in 1938 when oil promoter Jack Livingston gunned down his cousin, Purple Gang lawyer Isiah Leebove, over a land dispute. Isaiah's ghost is rumored to haunt the hotel, along with the original owner's wife, Helen Doherty (guests catch a whiff of her perfume). Shadowy figures have been spotted throughout the hotel. Also, the spirits of other murder victims roam the halls, locking and unlocking doors. Recently, a tunnel was found where the Purple Gang could escape the hotel unnoticed.

THE LOUNGE BAR, THE DOHERTY, CLARE, MICHIGAN

E-7265

HOTEL NORTHLAND — MARQUETTE, MICH.

DO NOT FORGET MARQUETTE. Now called the Landmark Inn—the Hotel Northland has had many famous guests since opening in 1930. Amelia Earhart stayed in Room 502, still named for her. Perhaps the Rolling Stones or Louis Armstrong saw the ghost of a librarian who stares out of the sixth-floor Lilac Room, waiting for her dead lover. The front desk gets calls from that room when no one is staying there.

OLDIE BUT GOODIE. The oldest hotel in the oldest city in Michigan, so how could it not be haunted? Since 1927, the Ojibway in Sault St. Marie has hosted queens, US presidents, and a few resident spirits, like Beatrice, the wife of a former owner. She has been known to rearrange things and even make the beds. A tall man in a top hat and tails has also been seen wandering the lobby.

HOTEL PANTLIND, GRAND RAPIDS, MICH.

GRAND AGAIN. The Beaux Arts–style of the Pantlind Hotel was one reason it was named "one of ten finest hotels in America" in 1925. Built in 1900 and remodeled in 1913, its ceiling still has the largest amount of gold leaf in America. This elegance was restored alongside a modern glass tower, and together, they became the Amway Grand Plaza in 1981. The ghosts are a bit like those in *The Shining*—they like to have a good time. A couple is frequently seen waltzing on the dance floor. A lost little boy wanders the hallways. There is even a spirit that empties dirty ashtrays—a shoo-in for "ghost employee of the year." The most famous and saddest story is of Mary Monko, a hotel worker who was decapitated in an elevator accident in 1914. It is said her spirit still rides the Grand's elevators.

CARRY ON. Carry Nation wielded her temperance ax on the liquor bottles at the Holly Hotel in 1908, and the place has been famous ever since. It has also had two fires exactly 65 years apart to the day. Luckily, the ghosts survived in what's considered the most haunted building in Michigan. The former owner of the hotel, a Mr. Hirst, has made his displeasure over renovations known, but he also laughs a lot. Nora Kane, a beautiful former hostess, occasionally plays the piano, and both she and her perfume waft through the house. The kitchen is very active, too, in addition to cooking delicious meals. Two little girls hang out there, one possibly killed in the nearby former livery stable. They play with the utensils and giggle. Other ghosts include a Native American man, a cigar smoker, and a dog.

TERRACE INN. BAY VIEW. MICH.

ROOMS WITH A VIEW. The charming Terrace Inn is part of the classic Victorian community of Bay View. Two workers were killed in the 1910 construction, and it is said that they still wander their old place of employment. A lady in white has been seen searching for her husband, Edward, who dresses in tweed. There is even a ghost file at the front desk, for those who wish to add to their stories.

BUSY BODIES. It survived two fires, yet the hauntings persist. The South Lyon Hotel was built in 1867, but strange things happen when one's location is over an old cemetery. The bodies were moved, but they never really left. Now a restaurant, the ladies restroom upstairs is particularly haunted, with women hearing footsteps and doors slamming when no one else is there. Ghostly children have been heard and seen as well.

THE JOINT IS STILL JUMPING. With a history of being a blues club, a bordello, and a speakeasy during Prohibition, the former Lamar Hotel/ Horseshoe Bar has a wonderfully checkered past. It even has a secret room. Built as a Grand Rapids railroad hotel in 1891, it now houses retail businesses. However, all sorts of odd things continue to happen: noises, strange handprints, and the presence of a small child.

VERY OLD SOULS. When one dines at Perry's Schuch Hotel, one of the oldest restaurants in the country, they are in good company—well, at least spooky company. This Saginaw landmark started as a hotel in 1868. Although no longer a place to sleep, the third floor still is active. Paranormal groups have seen flying objects and heard strange voices saying, "Help me," and faces are seen in the upstairs windows.

BEWARE THE LADY IN RED. Built in 1835, Marshall's National House Inn is one of Michigan's finest bed and breakfasts. Coauthor Milan checked in once and matter-of-factly asked the clerk if it was haunted. Initially, the clerk said no, but while showing Milan to his room, he admitted the last tenants left that morning at 3:00 a.m.—the couple woke to a ghost standing in the doorway looking at them.

COURTING GHOSTS. A stagecoach stop along the old Grand River Trail, the 1836 Botsford Inn was where Henry Ford courted his wife, Clara. He bought it and put springs in the floor of the ballroom upstairs. That is where odd things happened, with reports of dishes mysteriously moving and doors that would not open. A ghostly man has been spotted—perhaps Henry coming back to dance? Well-preserved, it is now an office building.

BOWERS HARBOR INN

PRESERVING THE PAST. Jealousy, an elevator, jam—it is all part of the legend of Genevieve Stickney, one of the most famous ghosts of Northern Michigan. Genevieve (or "Jennie") and her husband, Charles, built a big, beautiful home on the Old Mission Peninsula in 1927. Charles owned a canning company, and Genevieve loved serving her guests jellies and jams made from the plentiful fruit surrounding her. While those are facts, the haunted legends that sprang from the many rumors are still debated. It is said that Genevieve became so obese that her husband had to install an elevator in their home. Then, he had to hire a nurse to take care of her. Genevieve grew jealous of this nurse and suspected Charles of having an affair with her. That jealousy proved fatal.

Where There's a Will, There's a "Hey!" When Charles died, he left his entire fortune to the nurse—and the inn to Genevieve. Despondent, she hung herself in the elevator shaft. Yet, Genevieve still very much lives at the inn. Her reflection, in period dress, has been known to show up in her gilt-edged mirror in the hallway as well as the ladies' room, startling women visitors. Of course, the elevator seemed to have a life of its own, with strange noises and movement at all hours. Faucets and lights turn themselves on and off randomly. Sometimes, even a blurry image of a woman shows up in guests' photographs. The inn no longer is a hotel but is home to the Mission Table and Jolly Pumpkin Restaurants, which feature Michigan-centric dishes. They also host many events. Guests are always hoping Genevieve will show up for tea and jam. (Courtesy of Mission Restaurant Group.)

GHOSTS IN GENERAL. Mysterious murders, money grabbing, and the ghost of Martha Mulholland all are part of the well-known ghost stories of Dixboro. The Dixboro General Store, built in 1840, still proudly stands to tell them. The owners have their own ghost who occasionally knocks things over yet is helpful around the store. In fact, the ghost actually once put price stickers on their still-crated jars of jam and jellies. Could it be the ghost of Martha, who was poisoned by her greedy brother-in-law James in 1845? James's wife, Anna, died under mysterious circumstances as well. Martha's son later took in boarders who repeatedly saw the ghost of Martha wearing white and moaning, "James has got it all." The same might be said of the general store, which has everything from penny candy to garden accents.

Four

LIGHTHOUSES, SHIPWRECKS, AND LOST ON THE LAKES

SHADOWY SHIPS AND SENTINELS. Surrounded by Great Lakes with more than 120 lighthouses (the most in the United States), it is no surprise shipwrecks and nautical disasters are a major part of Michigan history. According to the Great Lakes Shipwreck Museum at Whitefish Point (at right), more than 6,000 ships and 30,000 lives have been lost on the lakes since 1679. It is little wonder there are so many accounts of Flying Dutchmen and haunted lighthouses.

"Danger, Will Robinson." White River Light has stood where the channel empties into Lake Michigan since 1875. Prior to that, Capt. William Robinson posted a lantern to aid navigation. He eventually became the keeper when the lighthouse became a reality. Serving 50 years, he died in 1919 but never gave up the ghost. Though the light is now a museum, he is still regularly heard climbing the stairs, his lantern still seen late at night.

Doom on the Range. Lighthouse hauntings with black widow mysteries can have "illuminating" conclusions. Julia Brown became a keeper of the Saginaw River Range Light when her husband died suddenly in 1873. When she married George Way, she was subsequently demoted and eventually replaced. George also met an untimely end. Since then, residents and visitors regularly report footsteps on the stairs and voices coming from the tower. (Courtesy of Leslie Gregory.)

OLD SAILORS NEVER DIE. Moored in Bay City, the USS *Edson* saw action in Vietnam before becoming the Saginaw Valley Naval Ship Museum. Though officially retired, some crew members seem to remain on "active" duty. Gerald Hunter reports overhearing ghostly conversations on board, and many report tools being moved, strange voices, and vacant cars mysteriously starting in the lot. The ship has even been featured on ghost-hunting television programs.

LITTLE GIRL LOST. Of all lighthouse hauntings, perhaps the eeriest is a solitary little girl visible on clear days, standing in the window of the Marquette Harbor Light, silently staring out over Lake Superior. She is a familiar sight, and one longtime employee remarked, "You can't help wonder who she must have been, and what she's looking for out there. Perhaps she's looking for her parents, and wondering what has happened to everyone." (Courtesy of the Library of Congress.)

MINNIE QUAY. So goes the final stanza of the *Ballad of Minnie Quay:* "Minnie Quay is not at rest, or so the people say / Her ghost still walks the lonely shore / Some see her to this day." In 1876, the 15-year-old Mary Jane "Minnie" Quay fell in love with a Great Lakes sailor who frequented Forester—a tiny Lake Huron village 35 miles north of Port Huron. Word got around fast in that small community, and Quay's age, coupled with the reputation of sailors, made for a scandal. Once the affair was exposed, her parents forbade her to see the young man and locked her in her room. Unable to make their nightly rendezvous, the ill-fated couple would never see one another alive again. More than 100 years later, the Tanner Inn (below) still stands silent witness to the tragedy.

LOST IN THE GALE. Within days, news came to Forester that the young sailor had perished, along with all hands, in a Lake Huron gale. Devastated, Quay left her infant brother unattended one April morning and headed for the Lake Huron dock. Guests at the Tanner Inn reported seeing her silently walk the length of the pier before plunging to her death in the icy waters. Today, all that remains of the dock are the rotting pylons (above), but for more than a century, people have reported seeing her ghost walking along the shore. It is said that her ghostly spirit has lured more than one young girl to her death in the lake. Her grave (below) is just up the road in the Quay family plot, Forester Township Cemetery.

LEAVE A LIGHT ON. With such isolation and harsh conditions, lighthouses are home to haunted tales—particularly the old and new Presque Isle lighthouses near Alpena. The old (1840) lighthouse (at left) is one of the oldest surviving lights on the Great Lakes. Various stories about a lightkeeper's wife abound; whether her husband locked her up or she became insane from loneliness, her shrieks can still be heard. But it is also haunted in a rather stunning way. Even though the lighthouse was decommissioned and has no source of power or even a lens, on some nights its light has been seen shining brightly over Lake Huron. About a mile north, the new (1870) light (below) is the tallest lighthouse on the Great Lakes that the public can climb and also rumored to be haunted. Both lighthouses are now museums truly worth visiting.

LONG DAY'S JOURNEY TO THE LIGHT. James S. Donahue lost a leg in the Civil War, but that did not stop him from becoming the South Haven lightkeeper, in 1874. Despite the fact the original light had a 75-foot walkway, Donahue maintained a reputation for tirelessly attending to his duties in any weather, for more than 35 years, and is credited with saving many lives. Things became more difficult with the 1903 light (below), set further out and accessed via an elevated catwalk, but Donahue never wavered; perhaps that is why he is still at it. Today, the keeper's house (above) is a museum where employees and visitors report the strange, unmistakable sound of Donahue hobbling around the second floor and banging crutches along the stairway. Other unexplained sounds and voices are also reported, and doors often open on their own.

Point Gratiot Light House, Port Huron, Mich.

CALLING ALL GHOST HUNTERS. The Fort Gratiot Lighthouse near Port Huron (1828) is Michigan's oldest. The still-active light has been restored and is open to the public. Over the past few years, it has also welcomed regularly scheduled paranormal investigations (also open to the public), hosted by Canton-based Motor City Ghost Hunters (MCGH). The light has been considered haunted for generations and, over a series of investigations, the MCGH have reportedly encountered a number of entities, including a small child and the ghost of a former lightkeeper. The group utilizes a variety of tools in their investigations for measuring electromagnetic wave activity, detecting unusual spikes in temperature, and making audio and video records in hopes of capturing paranormal activity and to facilitate post-investigation research. Many EVP have been captured at the Fort Gratiot light, and many are available online. (Above, courtesy of the Library of Congress.)

THE GHOSTLY CAPTAIN OF CAT'S HEAD POINT. The Grand Traverse Light (1858) is located in Leelanau State Park, where visitors can stop by or volunteer for a two-week stint as a keeper, working alongside the ghost of Capt. Peter Nelson (1811–1892). He's been encountered by many, sometimes standing in doorways kicking off his boots or overheard, muttering and noisily mounting the stairs to the light. The Captain is considered a warm, welcoming presence.

TO THE LIGHTHOUSE. The Point Iroquois Light at Brimley overlooks the scene of a bloody 17th-century battle between Ojibwe and Iroquois warriors. Ghostly shadows seen near the lighthouse are said to be their restless spirits. Visitors also report seeing the ghost of a little girl who was killed and eaten by a bear long ago. When the bear was hunted down and killed, parts of her body were discovered inside.

GOOD CHOICE. On the rocky shores of Lake Michigan, Seul Choix ("only choice" in French) was so named because it was the only safe refuge for sailors in that area—at least a dozen shipwrecks occurred nearby. Considered one of Michigan's most haunted lighthouses, its most famous keeper was Capt. Joseph Willie Townsend, who tended from 1902 to 1910. When he died, his body was embalmed and lay in the parlor for three weeks. Some say he never left. An avid cigar smoker, many still smell pungent smoke throughout the nonsmoking building. Silverware gets rearranged overnight, with fork tines pointing down as the English captain preferred. Upstairs, faces are seen in mirrors. There have been many sightings of Captain Townsend. Some visitors have even thought he was a tour guide—only to watch him disappear.

THE HOLY GRAIL OF SHIPWRECKS. In 1679, French explorer LaSalle sailed his 45-ton barque, *Le Griffon*, onto the Great Lakes. During its maiden voyage, it sailed to an island near Green Bay, loaded with furs, set on its return—and then disappeared. It has never been found, but for centuries, its ghostly form has been reported, silently sailing by in the thickest fog and the darkest of moonless nights.

THE GRIFFIN.

From an old cut.

FLYING DUTCHMAN OF LAKE SUPERIOR. On November 21, 1902, the great, Canadian steel-hulled steamer *Bannockburn* disappeared with all hands on Lake Superior. She has never been found; only an oar and life jacket somewhere near the Stannard's Rock Light have been retrieved. Since then, sightings of the *Bannockburn* far outnumber sightings of any other ghost ship, and sailors have long considered its sighting to be a bad omen. (Both, courtesy of Keith M. Steffke, SMMC.)

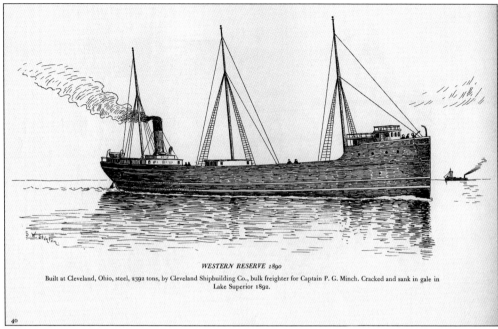

WESTERN RESERVE 1890

Built at Cleveland, Ohio, steel, 2392 tons, by Cleveland Shipbuilding Co., bulk freighter for Captain P. G. Minch. Cracked and sank in gale in Lake Superior 1892.

40

THE WESTERN RESERVE AND THE W.H. GILCHER. On August 30, 1892, the *Western Reserve* (above) broke in two and sank in the waves of a stormy Lake Superior. With the exception of the wheelsman, the wreck claimed all hands, including the ship's builder, Peter Minch (great-grandfather of George Steinbrenner) and much of his family. Since then, the phantom ship has regularly been spotted near Deer Park, though her broken hull lies 594 feet below the surface. Great Lakes ship historian and archivist Keith M. Steffke says its sister ship, the *W.H. Gilcher* (below), another of the famed lake phantoms, sank two months later in the deep waters of Lake Michigan. Like the *Western Reserve*, an apparition of the *Gilcher* is often reported in the fog near the straits of Mackinac. (Both, courtesy of Keith M. Steffke, SMMC.)

GREAT LAKES STEAMSHIP W. H. GILCHER, 1892.

62

THE TRIANGLE AND DRUM. A triangular area roughly extending from Ludington to Manitowoc, Wisconsin, and down to St. Joseph is known as the Great Lakes Triangle, claiming more ships and planes than the Bermuda Triangle. North of here, from Lakes Michigan to the distant expanses of Huron, is the region of the Ottawa Drum. The mysterious booming sound often heard from somewhere across the lake is said to be tolling the dead. (Courtesy of the Library of Congress.)

Copyright 1905 by the Rotograph Co.
H 7620 U. S. Light House, Escanaba, Mich.

Handcolored.

ESUOHTHGIL REDRUM. The ghost of Mary Terry is said to haunt the Sand Point Light near Escanaba. She became its first keeper in 1868 after her husband died before the light was completed. She served 18 years and died under mysterious circumstances when the light caught fire in 1886. Signs of forced entry led authorities to suspect she was killed by a burglar who tried to hide the crime by setting the blaze.

MORE GEORGE. George Foreman can relate to the Eagle Harbor Lighthouse in the Keweenaw Peninsula; three of the former keepers were named George. None of them like rock music. They will turn off the radio, crash dresser drawers on the ground, and generally make a lot of noise. In the 1850s-era Lake Breeze Lodge next door, a ghostly woman often appears on the porch, looking for her husband lost at sea. (Courtesy of the Library of Congress.)

STAY AT THE BAY. The Big Bay lighthouse, overlooking Lake Superior, is also a bed and breakfast. Visitors may catch a glimpse of red-headed William Prior, the original keeper, who hanged himself after the death of his assistant-keeper son. A soldier stationed there in 1952 was arrested for the murder of a local tavern owner; that story is the basis for the book and movie *Anatomy of a Murder.*

Five

MANITOUS, CURSES, PHANTOM LIGHTS, AND RED DWARFS

THE DROWNING POOL OF MACKINAC ISLAND. Beyond Arch Rock (above) lies an infamous stretch of water. During the 18th century, it is believed seven women drowned here, victims of witch trials. Tied to rocks and cast into Lake Huron, their verdicts were determined by their fate—if they floated, they were witches, and if they drowned, they were innocent. Even today, tourists report seeing hovering apparitions and hearing terrified screams.

SEEING RED. The harbinger of Detroit doom dates back to 1701, when city founder Antoine de la Mothe Cadillac had a dream about a red dwarf. A fortune teller told him to appease the "Nain Rouge" if he ever encountered him. But when Cadillac saw the fearsome eyes and pointed teeth of the red imp, he struck him with his cane. The Nain Rouge then cursed Cadillac, which resulted in him returning to France, going to jail, and losing his fortune. Later, the Nain began appearing in Detroit to warn about impending disasters: the 1763 Battle of Bloody Run, the devastating 1805 fire, the 1967 uprising, and even as recently as a bad 1976 snowstorm. Each spring, there is a creative parade that celebrates the Nain Rouge legend, but be careful if you see him.

LOVE BEFORE YOU LEAP. This 145-foot-high limestone pillar is one of Mackinac Island's most famous sites, seen here in an 1855 stereoscope. A Native American maiden named Michi leaped to her death after her father murdered her lover. She cursed the tribe and the island; perhaps that is why visitors tend to overindulge on fudge.

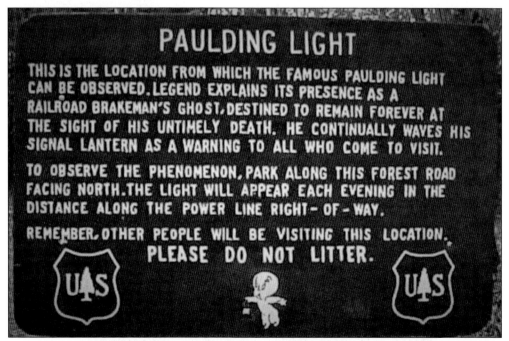

LIGHT FANTASTIC. It has baffled even the experts. The Paulding Lights near Watersmeet are unique. A mysterious light appears every night near the railroad tracks. Legends include a phantom brakeman who was killed trying to stop an oncoming train—the light is his lantern. *Ripley's Believe It or Not!* once offered $100,000 to anyone who could solve this. It is one of the few phenomena recognized by the National Park Service.

LONESOME WAIL. In 1907, railroad employees and their families boarded a train in Ionia, bound for a company picnic. Crossing into Salem over the curved Van Sickle Cut, they collided with a northbound freight. A total of 34 were killed, and hundreds were injured in Michigan's worst rail disaster. It is said the Van Sickle Cut, stretching from Five Mile to Napier, is still haunted by the sound of the terrible crash and the harrowing screams of passengers.

WARLOCK'S GRAVE. Near Dexter, along Huron River Drive, Old Scio Cemetery lies in ruins. In 1840, Robert Seymour was buried here beside a thorn tree. Today, in what historian Wystan Stevens referred to as the "wisdom of high school students," the unmarked plot is the legendary Warlock's Grave, a supposed "portal," possessing supernatural powers—one hopes it can command curious teens to bring a rake along to help save the cemetery.

Six

THEATERS, OPERA HOUSES, AND MOVIE PALACES

PHANTOMS OF THE OPERA HOUSES. Countless Michigan towns proudly boast of beautifully restored, concert halls, opera houses, and movie palaces. Many have featured some of the greatest performers and lecturers in history. While the shows may have come and gone, there are a few where the performances (and audience members) have been held over—eternally. Coldwater's Tibbits Opera House (1882) has been investigated by paranormal groups, and several EVP have been recorded.

1911 Calumet Theatre and Town Hall.

A Town Remembers. Calumet was the center of the Upper Peninsula's 19th-century copper mining industry. Its grand opera house opened in 1900 and hosted many theater luminaries, such as John Philip Sousa and Sarah Bernhardt. But it is a Polish Shakespearean actress that is its most famous ghost: Madame Helena Modjeska. Her ghost is still seen from the stage, helpfully mouthing lines when actors forget them. And a tragedy still haunts this theater. On Christmas Eve 1913, striking mining workers and their families were having a party in the nearby Italian Hall. Someone yelled, "Fire," and the stampede to exit resulted in 73 deaths, 59 of them children. There was no fire, and no one was ever charged with the crime. The opera house was used as a makeshift morgue, and some still hear the ghosts of the dead children. (Left, courtesy of Michigan Technological University Archives and Copper Country Historical Collections.)

HART AND SOULS. The Hartland Music Hall was originally a church. Now, the 1858 building holds musical performances and plays. In fact, during a performance of *The Mousetrap*, a fake prop clock actually chimed. Neighbors hear organ music when no one is in the building. And a ghostly music lover appears in the balcony, wearing a pearl necklace. The nearby cemetery has its own tales of orbs, disembodied voices, and misty figures.

FINE SHRINE. The Temple Theater in Saginaw was built for vaudeville by Shriners in 1927. The beautiful 1,750-seat theater was facing demolition, and, luckily, renovated in 2002. During the renovation, tools would move, orbs appeared, and a piano would start playing when no one was there. The chandeliers still go on and off randomly. There is also a haunted patron who is unhappy when someone sits in his seat.

CAPITOL IDEA. One of the happiest stories in this book, the Capitol Theater in Flint has recently been restored to its 1928 splendor. Architect John Eberson's style was to design theaters to look like European courtyards. One can see why the ghosts never wanted to leave. Uniformed ushers, workmen in 1920s-style clothing, and pale patrons in the balcony have been spotted when no one was supposed to be in the building. Many musicians, including members of AC/DC and Ray Charles, have played here and experienced strange things. Equipment failures, unexplained singing from various places in the theater, and knocking on walls during sound checks have all disturbed people. There is even a glowing little girl who appears onstage from time to time. No matter who is on screen or stage, scheduled or not, the Capitol is worth a trip to Flint.

HOWELL ROARS. It was an infirmary for Civil War soldiers, but now the 1928 Howell Theater is home to movies, parties, and some unusual ghosts, according to the Portal Paranormal Society. A little boy has been seen in the projection booth. Some have seen a ghostly lion (not the MGM one) charge at them. Rumor has it that circus animals are buried nearby. (The authors highly recommend this venue.) (Courtesy of Duane Zemper.)

VITAL ORGAN. The Redford Theater in Detroit featured an unusual Japanese theme when it opened in 1928 but that was painted over during World War II. Volunteers restored the Redford back to its glory, including the original Barton organ, and continue to host classic movies and concerts. The dressing room is reportedly haunted, as are several seats. Even the ladies room has a ghost—a volunteer who used to clean it.

ALL TALK, SOME ACTION. Since the 1970s, the former Michigan Theater has had a name that is slightly harder to pronounce: now it is the Frauenthal Center for the Performing Arts. This restored 1,725-seat Spanish–style "100% all-talking motion pictures" theater is lovingly haunted by the man who built it in 1930, at the cost of $690,000. The dapper impresario P.J. Schlossman makes his ghostly presence known by pushing down seats, opening and closing doors, and generally hanging out in his theater. Patrons have also reported seeing a small figure in black who appears in odd places. Although his ghost is not here, there is a statue of Buster Keaton nearby. Keaton spent his childhood summers in Muskegon, and every year, there is a festival at the Frauenthal dedicated to his films.

GOOD COMPANY. Whispers and laughter coming from the audience are common at the Beckwith Theater in Dowagiac—when no one is there. Props are moved and sometimes hidden. The spirit of a little girl roams the 19th-century theater. She is thought to have been left behind by an orphan train during the Depression. If one attends a play here, perhaps they will meet.

GOIN' TO JACKSON. Groucho Marx and Bob Hope came to Jackson's Michigan Theater, a grand Spanish-style 1930 movie palace that still shows films, plays, and concerts. Upon visiting, be on the lookout for the transparent woman in the balcony who sometimes stays late. Phantom ushers have whispered in patrons' ears and touched their shoulders. Also, watch out for the little girl who runs around upstairs when the theater is empty.

On with the Show. What was once the showplace of Howell, Michigan, is returning to its glory years. The Howell Opera House was built in 1881 at the cost of $11,000 and seated 800. The first play was *The Galley Slave*. This first-class venue was used by the community and the region for everything from plays to graduation ceremonies. William Jennings Bryan, Henry Ford, and other speakers were featured here, along with light opera and Shakespeare. One of the most famous actresses of her time, Jessie Bonstelle, got her start here. The theater was closed in 1924 by the fire marshal and became storage for the variety of businesses on the first floor. The community has been renovating the opera house while uncovering relics of the past—and stirring up ghostly activity. Manager Sharon Fisher has many stories.

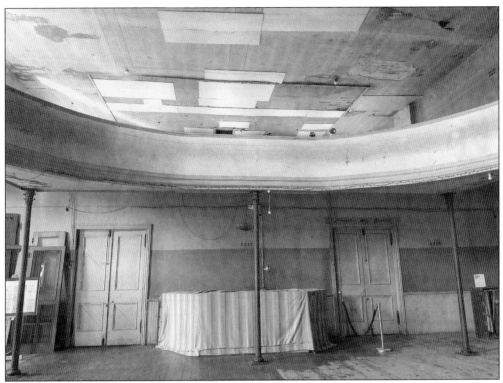

WORKING FOR PEANUTS. The resident ghost is a woman named Meredith. Apparently, she saw her husband attending the theater with another woman and stands in the balcony and cries. Another woman dressed in period clothing has been seen going up the steps to the balcony. A ghostly former ticket taker named Ralph is still on the job in what used to be the back office. Also, various children have been spotted on stage, with one clutching a cloth animal. There are sudden clouds of heavy perfume. Fisher even reports some visitors feel their hair being touched. While remodeling the balcony, old peanut shells were found under the seats—the origin of the term "peanut gallery." Sometimes, it takes over a hundred years to get a space back to its original use, but this one will be worth it.

Floyd Sat Here. This is another stunning theater comeback. Bay City's State Theater (built in 1908) was remodeled in 1930 by renowned architect C. Howard Crane, who also designed Detroit's Fox Theater. It had an unusual, colorful, Mayan Temple theme. In 2000, it almost became a parking lot but was saved by a dedicated group of volunteers and donors. They restored the original paintings on the ceiling and decorations throughout the theater itself. Sponsors purchased seats and put name plaques on them—including one for Floyd Ackerman, the former manager of the theater. Murdered in 1943, he is still seen, wearing black, in his favorite seat in the balcony near his office. Multitasking employee Brenda once heard loud voices in the lobby one night while closing up and found no one there, among other strange things.

Seven

CEMETERIES, PARKS, AND BATTLEFIELDS

BLOODY RUN. In 1763, during Pontiac's War, British soldiers attacked Chief Pontiac's men along Detroit's Parent Creek, now the site of Elmwood Cemetery. The surprise attack failed, and the British were badly beaten. So terrible was the slaughter, it is said the creek ran red with blood for days and was thereafter renamed Bloody Run Creek. Even today, apparitions of the dead soldiers are said to walk along its banks at twilight.

Who Is Minding the Museum? Built in 1833, the Detroit Arsenal was a walled fortress with 11 buildings; it stood in modern-day Dearborn. Today, two of the four remaining buildings are home to the Dearborn Historical Museum and considered actively haunted. People have long sensed a presence in the commandant's quarters (above), especially upstairs, where lights are sometimes observed through the windows long after hours. The McFadden-Ross House (below) was originally the powder magazine. It was converted to a private home after 1875. Both structures have been investigated by many groups, with surprising results. Among these are the Great Lakes Apparition Seekers and the Motor City Ghost Hunters. Using cameras and computer dowsing instruments, the group captured dialog in response to questions and even caught video footage of what they believe to be a ghostly occupant of the McFadden-Ross House.

Rest in Peace? Very close to Detroit, Ferndale's Machpelah Cemetery by day is a quiet, beautiful place. But late at night and early in the morning, neighbors have reported hearing bells and screaming coming from the back. People driving by on Woodward Avenue have seen weird smoky shapes gathering in parts of the cemetery.

Ghostly Gargling? No, but say "Maguaga," and someone might wonder. The Battle of Maguaga (also known as Monguagon) was a bloody 1812 skirmish near Trenton, where the apparition of a British soldier is often reported in the woods. According to legend, the ghost first appeared to his fiancé in Amherstburg, saying he was mortally wounded and describing where he lay. With a military escort, she found him later that day, exactly where described.

SECURE THE DOOR . . . QUICK! Few places are as ripe for haunting as historic Fort Wayne. Its construction, deemed necessary by disputes between Britain and Canada with the United States during the little-known Patriot War, began in 1843 along the Detroit River in the area known as the sand mounds of Springwells. Surrounded by more than 19 Native American burial mounds —one on the immediate grounds—the area has hosted human activity for over a thousand years. The massive, star-shaped fortress, walled in a labyrinth of brick and mortar tunnels with gun ports, was used as a training and mustering spot for soldiers during the Civil War and Spanish-American War, a detention center for suspected Communists during the Red Scare of the 1920s and a POW camp for Italian prisoners during World War II. Tales of hauntings predate the fort. (Above, courtesy of Library of Congress.)

A Ghost Hunter's Dream. That's
how Gerald Hunter describes Fort
Wayne. His investigation, accompanied
by members of the Metro Paranormal
Society, is detailed in *Haunted Michigan
3: The Haunting Continues*. In an
overnight investigation, Hunter and
crew encountered an incredible amount
of paranormal activity, especially in
the limestone barracks, where he and
assistant Sarah listened in amazement
(at 3:30 a.m.) as a ghostly sentry unit
was ordered to "secure the door" and
responded with "closing the door." In
addition, ghostly figures were captured
on film; one amazing photograph
featured a soldier who appeared after
the film was developed. Subsequent
employee interviews also uncovered
fascinating encounters, including
apparitions of soldiers marching in
the yard, with one seen passing by a
window more than 12 feet above the
ground. Fort Wayne's a great place for
ghost hunters and history buffs alike.
(Both, courtesy of Library of Congress.)

REMEMBER THE RAISIN! On January 22, 1813, British troops and forces of the Tecumseh Confederation attacked American militia at Frenchtown on the River Raisin, near Monroe. The Americans were badly beaten, losing 397 men. More than 500 were taken prisoner and forced to march to Canada. The next day, many of those left behind were massacred by the confederation. Afterward, a warning went out that anyone attempting to aid the fallen would be killed. The dead were left where they fell, and they remain there to this day, flesh and bone slowly swallowed by the swampy soil. Years later, a paper mill was built over the graves, and subsequent contamination still prevents disinterment. No wonder the River Raisin Battlefield, Michigan's newest National Park, is also one of the state's top-10 paranormal sites, where sightings of ghostly apparitions are regularly reported.

WALK, DON'T RUN . . . ON SECOND THOUGHT, RUN! Westland's William Ganong Cemetery is considered one of our most haunted. Established in 1832, it is nestled on a dark hill along a forgotten stretch of Henry Ruff Road. It was once famously visited by the late Gundella the Witch (also known as Marion Kucla), a self-proclaimed psychic and author, who was often featured on local radio and TV programs. Several years ago, she claimed to have found a blonde woman's scalp there, perhaps related to the "Woman in White," the ghostly apparition thought responsible for several auto accidents (some fatal) occurring in front of the cemetery. In each incident, motorists ran off the road attempting to avoid a woman exiting the graveyard, running into the street. Always described as a blonde woman dressed in white, she disappears just as drivers swerve to avoid hitting her.

LADY AND CEMENT. Looking for the definition of "creepy-cool?" Try McCourtie Park in the Irish Hills. It is almost a secret, hidden among rolling hills and tall trees, where picturesque bridges span a quiet stream. Then, there are the abandoned cement pools, the crumbling hillside steps, and the unexplained building—complete with a series of windows and doors, like storefronts—built into the hill. Do not forget the realistic "trees" and "wooden" bridges made of molded concrete. To be fair, "What the heck is this place?" is not an uncommon reaction. If one is lucky enough to catch a glimpse of the "Woman in Blue," the ghostly lady often appearing near the hillside building, then welcome to McCourtie Park. Once the McCourtie family farmhouse and farm, it later became the estate of oil and cement tycoon William H.L. "Herb" McCourtie (1872–1933).

AIDEN LAIR. William McCourtie grew up here and, after making his fortune, transformed it into the opulent "Aiden Lair" estate. During the 1920s, he hosted parties and local events. Meanwhile, the hillside building included a rathskeller, where bootleg liquor was allegedly distilled, and private card parties were said to go on all night. Frequent guests included Henry Ford, Al Capone, and the Purple Gang. As for the concrete trees, they were actually well-disguised rathskeller chimneys. Hiring Mexican artisans, experts in a wet concrete process called El Trabejo Rustico (or Faux Bois), McCourtie commissioned a series of trees and bridges with shapes and surfaces that amazingly replicate wood, including bark, grain, and etchings of burrowing insects. Today, these are among Michigan's greatest surviving examples of the craft. Though the parties ended long ago, the ghost of the lady in blue still lingers.

GATED COMMUNITY. Canton's Kinyon Cemetery sits along an unspoiled stretch of Ridge Road. It was established in 1840 on land donated by Orrin and Roxanne Kinyon. In 1849, Roxanne accidentally poisoned two of her children with horse medicine. The devastated woman visited their graves every day, and many still report the apparition of a woman walking among them. Paranormal investigations have captured several anomalies here, and many sense a strong mystical presence near the rare Native American modified trail tree, The nearby Kinyon house (below) is said to be haunted by the Kinyon children. This story is featured in *Ghost Stories and Other Tales from Canton*, Virginia Bailey Parker, Canton Historical Society, 1998; the home is listed in the National Register of Historic Places. The private residence is not open to the public.

Eight

HOMEBODIES AND MUNICIPAL MAYHEM

LOCATION, LOCATION, LOCATION. That cliché must be a standard in both worlds, and maybe that's why so many municipal buildings have ghostly residents. Wayne's Old Village Hall (built 1878) has been a firehouse, police station, and jail. Now a historical museum, it is a favorite of the Motor City Ghost Hunters. Their investigation found several resident spirits, including a drunken inmate and an old city employee. (There is no word on his state of mind.)

James Oliver Curwood Chateau, Owosso, Mich.

4408-29-N

J.O. Curwoods Studio Owosso, Mich.

CURWOOD'S CASTLE. James Curwood is still Owosso's most celebrated citizen. Born in 1878, he left high school early to attend the University of Michigan, then left to become a reporter and, by 1920, had become the highest paid adventure novelist of his time. In 1923, he built his dream house: a castle overlooking the Shiawassee River. He felt he had achieved everything and planned to live to 100, but he did not come close. His adventure ended at age 48, with a fatal spider bite. However, many say he never left the castle; in fact, three ghosts are said to be residing there. Over time, people have reported hearing strange voices and seeing faces peering from the windows. Today, it is a museum, and visitors still report odd noises and an eerie feeling of being watched. Several paranormal groups have led investigations here and have reported unusual sightings and collected EVP.

What Lies Beneath. The Hill was Plymouth's first cemetery. It was also an ancient, Indian burial mound. In 1846, the graves were allegedly relocated for the construction of the First Presbyterian Church; when it burned in 1936, excavation for a new church unearthed more than 40 human skeletons, with some barely below the surface. Perhaps this explains the man often seen wandering the lower level and strange voices heard down the dark, empty corridors.

Card-Carrying Spirits. This location is so haunted, a documentary was made about it. The castle-like limestone Hoyt Library has been serving Saginaw since 1890, when it was built on the site of an old jail. Maybe those former inmates are the ones throwing books from shelves. But it is also haunted by Harriet Ames, the first librarian, who hopefully puts them back. Perhaps visitors can see the little girl who wanders the former children's section.

Homey Spirit. It's no secret Plymouth's Our Lady of Good Counsel rectory has an extra spirit in residence. The house (above) belonged to state legislator Ebenezer Penniman (1804–1890), and it is pretty clear he's still there. He likes to knock on the second-story windows, ring the doorbell, and noisily rearrange books while priests are trying to sleep. Once, while repairing malfunctioning lights, a parishioner yelled, "Okay, Ebenezer, turn on the lights," and they immediately turned on.

Do Not Be Chicken. Part of the town since 1905, the Frankenmuth Historical Museum has been a hotel/saloon as well as a newspaper office. But a ghost, perhaps a former employee, hangs around the front. Attached is the 1894 Fischer Hall, site of the Notorious Flint Party of 1926. The *Frankenmuth News* described it as a "wild orgy" with "women dancers from Detroit" and 21 arrests. Ghost partiers may still be there.

JUST PASSING THROUGH. A spooky Saginaw sight, Potter Street Station is one of the largest Victorian train stations still (barely) standing in the United States. Many fallen soldiers passed through this station, and a local casket maker even had a shop in the depot. A woman in white has been seen by volunteers trying to restore the station. The film *A Haunting on Potter Street* captured a lot of paranormal activity.

GHOSTLY STATE. Lansing's Neoclassical Michigan State Capitol building's beauty came at a price. Finished in 1878 as one of the first domed capitols in the United States, the inside of the cast-iron dome features paintings of muses. Over the years, a painter and a roofer have fallen to their deaths, along with a page who missed the staircase. There have been ghostly sightings of the page and the painter. (Courtesy of the Library of Congress.)

Sorry, Wrong Number. In 1907, Warren and Virginia Randall moved into the Judd-White house in Grand Rapids. A short time later, Warren lost his leg in a work-related accident. Though fitted with a prosthetic limb, Warren was seriously depressed and suspected his wife of cheating. The newspapers claimed Warren beat Virginia to death with his artificial limb, then turned on the gas, and sliced his own throat with a razor. The incident shook the town; the house, rumored to be haunted, could not be sold. It was eventually demolished, and in 1924, the Michigan Bell Telephone Company erected an office building over the site. Since then, strange apparitions and odd events have been reported by employees. Over the years, many bizarre, late-night calls have been received by local residents, mysteriously traced back to the building.

PLAY, PAULINE. Ann Arbor's first grand piano was owned by Pauline and Reuben Kempf. This Greek Revival house they, and their Steinway piano, lived in was built in 1853. The Kempfs lived there from 1890 to 1953, teaching music to many local children. The Kempf house has been well preserved, with much of the original furniture. Pauline herself still haunts this beautiful place, occasionally playing a few notes.

DOWN BY THE OLD MILL SCREAM. The old mill in Dundee (1849) is now a museum but has served many purposes over the years—most notably as one of Henry Ford's village industry mills. While the source of the haunting is unclear, it is considered a highly active haunted site. Many EVP have been recorded here (some available online), and the public is invited to participate in regularly scheduled paranormal investigations.

TEMPLE OF ROOMS. The largest Masonic Temple in the world still towers over Detroit, keeping its secrets. The 1926 neo-Gothic building has over a thousand rooms. The building (originally planned to be shaped like a hammer) was designed by George D. Mason, who has reportedly returned in ghost form. He allegedly jumped off the 210-foot building after going bankrupt. That has been disputed, but some have seen his ghost climbing the stairs to the roof. Paranormal groups have explored the secret rooms and hidden passageways, finding much activity, like slamming doors, elevators running on their own, and even Masonic ghosts in uniform. Musicians from Jimi Hendrix to the Metropolitan Opera to Jack White have played here. And White had a theater named for him after he donated money to pay the tax bill, keeping the temple open.

HEART-FELT. Dorr Felt built his wife, Agnes, a beautiful mansion near Holland in 1928. Sadly, Agnes died not long after moving in, and Dorr followed soon after. But this love story has a happy ending: they are seen waltzing together in the ballroom and enjoying their house. Heavy doors open and shut on their own, and sometimes, Agnes even "slaps" someone with a blast of cold air if they behave badly.

CROOKS AND BOOKS. When a library is built on the site of a former jail, not everyone is into peace and quiet—especially because it is where Detroit's last public execution by hanging occurred. The Skillman branch of the Detroit Public Library is known for its strange noises, including moans, rumblings, and rattling chains. This beautiful 1932 building in downtown Detroit also houses the National Automotive History Collection.

ACTIVE ANTIQUARIANS. One of the most active haunted places is the Jackson Antiques Mall. Coauthor Milan has visited five times and experienced two encounters. Gerald Hunter's *More Haunted Michigan* details many mostly humorous experiences by employees and customers. While the 19th-century building has served many purposes, the most active ghost seems to be associated with the time it was a brothel. They call her Blanche, and it is believed she was the madam. Employees regularly report her clattering around in back while they are up front, even before opening. But she is not timid. She has assisted customers by snapping bracelet clasps for them and likes to rearrange stock and knock things off shelves. Once, a clerk and customer watched a ladder move away from a wall, only to return to where it was propped when the clerk yelled, "Blanche, put it back!"

PERSONAL SERVICE. When coauthor Jon Milan's son Evan was 10, the two stopped in to look around. Evan has always been sensitive to paranormal activity, so his father purposely avoided mentioning its haunted history. All was fine until they ascended the back stairs, where Evan uncharacteristically froze and loudly refused to go any further. Fifteen years later, Evan explained how he sensed something that filled him with a dread he did not care to encounter. On another occasion, Jon and his friend Christine were descending the basement steps when he playfully asked, "How's it going, Blanche?" The two were stunned when they both heard a woman reply "fine" in a voice that seemed to come from all around them. Other resident ghosts include a mustachioed man in a peacoat and a woman seen by passersby, peering out the upstairs window.

Too Bookish for a Boo Coup. John King Books, the "Second Best Bookstore in the World" (*Business Insider*), may be "Best in the Other World" as well. Boasting more than a million volumes, it is headquartered in Detroit, where two ghosts regularly roam the shelves. One is believed to be a woman who frequented the store. When she died, King bought her collection, and he says she has been haunting the third floor ever since. The fourth-floor ghost is more of a mystery—a timid fellow in vintage garb, he is often seen for a split second before disappearing. Both like to turn on reading lights late at night. In Grand Rapids, a ghost is often reported busily working in the basement of the Ryerson Library (below). It is thought to be the ghost of Grand Rapids Library director Samuel Ranck (1867–1952).

Booooooks! Lumber baron Charles Hackley gifted a public library to the people of Muskegon in 1890. In fact, he gave a third of his fortune to the city. Upon his death in 1905, he laid in state in his library. Patrons report sightings of Hackley still enjoying his library, particularly in the sitting room. Rumors abound that a ghost of a former employee floats between the stacks as well.

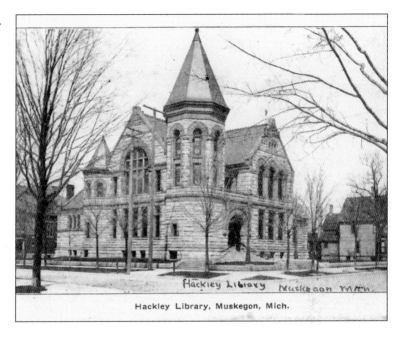

Hackley Library, Muskegon, Mich.

FIVE-ALARM HAUNTING. Fire chief Alonzo Miller was not at work when he died in 1940, but that would not keep a dedicated firefighter from active duty. Some say he is still haunting the place. Built in 1898, the Ypsilanti Firehouse is now the Michigan Firehouse Museum, a great place to learn about firefighting and investigate more than 70 years of banging, disembodied whispering, and lights and doors with a mind of their own.

FLINT'S FINEST. Banker Robert J. Whaley not only remodeled this beautiful Victorian house in 1885, but he also loaned "Billy" Durant $2,000 to start a road cart company that eventually became General Motors. Robert and his wife, Mary, were philanthropists and left legacies that still help Flint today. Those who tour the house will perhaps see a cloth that levitates (as seen by workmen) or shadowy figures. Mary sometimes appears, wandering the grounds.

BOCK LOVES BOOKS. A good bookstore is hard to find. The authors love the Olympia in Dowagiac— and so does a ghost named Mr. Bock, who likes to cause mischief in the store. He puts books in different places, sets off buzzers, and generally browses when no one is around. Sometimes he likes to drag a chair to the front door, looking out at the street from his former residence.

ROYAL HAUNT. Frank Henderson made a fortune in the uniform business and built a luxurious 25-room mansion in Kalamazoo in 1895. You can now stay in Henderson Castle, but you'd better be prepared for some company. Frank and his well-dressed wife, Mary, sometimes walk the halls. A Spanish-American War veteran is also occasionally on duty. There is even a ghost dog that may try to crawl into bed with visitors.

IN SESSION. The Livingston County Courthouse in Howell has been adjudicating since 1890. While most work has moved to a modern building, it still has a beautifully preserved courtroom. And it is spirit-friendly. People have reported seeing a blue-eyed woman with yellow hair in the hallways. Shadowy figures are seen in the windows late at night. Strange noises, knocks, and groans are heard by those who still work there.

Ladies Library, Ypsilanti, Mich.

ALL DAY, ALL NIGHT, MARYANNE. The Ypsilanti Ladies Library (built 1858) began as home to Maryanne Starkweather, an important community force and philanthropist with a progressive eye. When she died in 1890, it was donated to the Ladies Library Association. An obsessive micromanager, there is little wonder Starkweather's stern figure was often seen on the upper floors. Today, it is primarily used as commercial office space where tenants still see and hear her.

"MUTH" MEANS COURAGE. The town of Frankenmuth and St. Lorenz Lutheran Church both began in 1845. They still have a monthly service almost entirely in German. One can see a replica of the original log church near to the current, impressive Gothic one, built in 1880. The cemetery attached to the "modern" church is the site of a legless woman who has been seen floating over the gravestones at night.

DOA. The Detroit Institute of Arts (DIA) is a world-class museum that art lovers even appreciate by night. Security guards regularly hear loud thuds echoing through the halls. In the African Art Gallery, the 19th-century "Nail Figure" has been observed moving and even dancing. Loud crashes have been heard in the gallery where *The Court of Death* painting hangs. It's as if something has fallen—yet everything is in place.

SCHVITZ FITS. A mainstay of the Detroit North End, the Russian-style Schvitz opened in 1930. The bathhouse was a gathering place—and a safe hangout for the Purple Gang. They could take a steam and relax without packing heat. However, they did leave bullet holes in a painting. The spirited presence of former "schvitzers" is definitely felt in the beautifully tiled rooms. Still open, the Schvitz is restored and thriving.

No Ghosts Barred Here! The Whitney is a wonderful restaurant that embraces its ghostly history. It even has a Ghostbar. Built in 1894 for lumber baron David Whitney and his wife, Flora, the 21,000-square-foot mansion has Tiffany windows throughout. It cost $400,000 to build, about $9.5 million today. Flora died before it was finished. David then married Flora's sister Sara, and that is when the haunting began. Flora's ghost wanders, despondent that her sister lived in her dream house. Ghost hunters have seen floating lights and other paranormal activity. The elevator stops at every floor after hours when no one is there. The staff also reports seeing apparitions and wandering spirits—perhaps former patrons—and silverware that moves on its own. Why not have dinner in the lovely drawing room or the Ghostbar and find out?

Nine

GREENFIELD VILLAGE AND HENRY FORD

WHO YA GONNA CALL? Some places embrace their haunted heritage, while others prefer keeping it quiet. At the Henry Ford Museum and Greenfield Village, paranormal activity is common though seldom publicized. While most occur in the village, the museum is not exempt. Over the years, many claim to have glimpsed President Kennedy standing beside this limousine in which he took his final ride, only to find no one there.

HOUSE OF HENRY. Here is where the Ford empire began: Henry Ford was born in this farmhouse in 1863. It originally stood at the corner of what is now Greenfield and Ford Roads in the former Greenfield Township. This is one of the first buildings seen in Greenfield Village. Ford moved it here in 1944. He meticulously filled it with period furniture; it took him 18 months just to find the exact kind of stove he grew up with. One of the few original pieces was his mother's spinning wheel—now gone, it was frequently seen spinning on its own. Clearly, Ford still feels at home here. The rocking chair starts rocking when no one is near, and books move. And the door to the home locks and unlocks by itself. Village guides definitely feel a presence moving through the house.

THE WRIGHT STUFF. One of the most notoriously haunted dwellings in the park is the Wright Brothers home. It is where Wilbur and Orville grew up, and Wilbur died in 1912. Many refuse to work in the house, and guides can recount haunted happenings (off the record, of course). A common occurrence is the man in a dark suit and dress shoes often seen descending the stairs. Guides and cleaning staff often see him, and he sometimes stops to regard them before walking through to the kitchen. Conversation and footsteps are often heard coming from the roped-off second story. A few years ago, when the house was closed for renovation, workmen were repeatedly locked out when attempting to re-enter following lunch. Yet, they had been eating outside, next to the house, and no one else had approached the house.

GO TOWARD THE LIGHT. Bringing Thomas Edison's Menlo Park, New Jersey, laboratory to Greenfield Village was Henry Ford's passion project. In fact, for years, the museum and village were known as the Edison Institute. Not only did Ford have the 1876 lab meticulously set up exactly as Edison had, but he also brought in dirt from the surrounding yard for additional authenticity. All of Edison's early experiments were conducted (pun intended) here. His office, library, and machine shop are also on view. Edison's engineers are still hard at work. Guides report hearing footsteps going up the stairs and walking around the lab when there are no visitors in the building and doors opening and closing. In 1920, Edison told *Scientific American* magazine that he was working on a machine that could speak to the dead—a variation on his phonograph.

THEY ALL BOUGHT THE FARM. The Susquehanna House was originally thought to date from 17th-century Maryland (but later attributed to about 1830), a plantation home that thrived on the fruits of slave labor. Perhaps that's why the heavy footsteps heard tromping across the porch are so unsettling to guides. They seem darkly threatening—the tread of an intolerant overseer? Fortunately, whenever guides look on the porch, no one is there. On better days, they hear the ghostly sounds of children playing coming from the yard out back. Over at the Daggett farmhouse (below), all the spirits seem comforting, even helpful. One caught a guide as she fell down the stairs, allowing her to reclaim her footing on the steps. The ghosts are thought to include Samuel Daggett (the smell of his pipe smoke lingers), a little girl, and a boarder.

EAVESDROPPING AND TAG. The lesser-known Giddings House dates from 1751. While furnished in Colonial style, visitors can only enter the first- and second-floor landings, the rooms visible through glass. On the "Passion for the Past" blog, one former guide recalls using the bathroom behind the structure after hours and overhearing voices from within. At first, he thought it was recorded narration but soon realized it was an actual conversation. It stopped, briefly, but as he left, he overheard the voice say, "He's leaving now." The 350-year-old Cotswold Cottage (below) has a few skeletons in its own closet—or storage area, rather. While some guides avoid the place, one tells of seeing a dark shadowy form leaping out of a corner, bolting toward her, and then going right through her—It's no surprise she left in a hurry.

WHOA, NOAH! Noah Webster wrote his dictionary in this impressively large house near Yale University (it was later used as a dormitory). Published in 1828, the *American Dictionary of the English Language* was the first truly American collection of words. The Webster house, built in 1823, was brought to the Village from New Haven, Connecticut, in 1936. Upstairs, Noah himself is said to walk the halls and even hang out in some of the rooms. Guides regularly hear footsteps coming from the upper floors when no one else is in the house. Even a little boy once talked about the nice man he met upstairs, when, of course, no one was there. Sometimes, horses refuse to walk past the house or get spooked—what are they seeing?

TAVERN ON THE GREEN(FIELD). The former Clinton Inn (above), built in 1831, offered food and lodging to travelers along US Route 12, also known as the Old Chicago Road. In 1927, it changed its name and location when Henry Ford put it in his new venture: Greenfield Village (below). The dilapidated building was remodeled and became a public dining room renamed the Eagle Tavern, where Henry celebrated his 79th birthday in 1942. What he did not realize is that it still had a few unexpected tenants. There have been sightings of a man and a woman hanging out in the bar area, dressed in 19th-century clothes. People think they are costumed guides at the Village, yet when approached, the "barflies" disappear, sometimes right into the walls. The Eagle Tavern still serves hungry travelers. Many menu items are made from 19th-century recipes.

GHOST OR NO GHOST. The Logan County Courthouse (above) is considered haunted, but some ghosts aren't what they appear. In *The People's Tycoon*, published by Vintage Books in 2006, author Steven Watts writes how Henry Ford once hired a Lincoln look-alike to work there. One night, the actor fell asleep in Lincoln's chair, and an after-hours security guard discovered him. Convinced he had seen a ghost, the guard turned in his badge and quit. Less explainable are the strange lights that appear in the upstairs windows from time to time. Though they seem to go on and off at all hours, no one's ever found inside. Another home of paranormal interest is the 1816 Vienna, Ontario, home of Thomas Edison's grandparents (below). Seemingly a peaceful country farmhouse, guides have experienced seasick-like dizziness near the fireplace and observed the shadow of a man walking through the parlor.

THE MEN UPSTAIRS. Inspired by New England churches and named for Henry Ford's mother Mary and mother-in-law Martha, the nondenominational Martha Mary Chapel was built in 1929. The bell was cast in Boston in 1834 by Paul Revere's son Joseph. The ghost of Henry Ford himself has been seen in the balcony, as well as reports of some unexplained singing during services. One of the first buildings in the country to be wired for electricity, the Sarah Jordan Boarding House (below) was the New Jersey home to employees of Thomas Edison. The 1870 house has many of the Jordan family's original furnishings. One of the former boarders feels right at home. A guide reported seeing a bearded man wearing suspenders staring out of the third-floor window in a room that is kept locked and off-limits.

TREAD LIGHTLY. Ohio was the tire industry birthplace, and this is where the Firestone brand was born. The Firestone Farm, built in 1828, was moved from Columbus. Harvey Firestone grew up here, working for a buggy company before making his future on the wheels. Now the farm shows what 19th-century farm life was like. It is also one of the most haunted places in the village. There are a lot of unexplained thumping noises, especially on the stairs, and a ghost named Sally creaks the rocking chair upstairs and sometimes looks out the window. Women's voices are heard in the kitchen when the building is empty. Sally is also known for drinking any coffee the guides leave around. The Firestone Barn (below) is also haunted by a man said to have committed suicide there.

Have You Ridden a Ford Lately? William Ford built this barn in 1863 on his Greenfield Township property. It was modified when it was put into the village and, today, is used as stables for the carriage horses. People have heard ghost horses stampeding in the barn when no live horses are in there.

Leave It. Henry Ford's funeral procession somberly wound through Greenfield Village in April 1947. His body then lay in state in Lovett Hall (above). Named after Ford's favorite dance instructor, it features a large ballroom upstairs with a spring-mounted floor. Events are still held here. Once, a server encountered a group of ghostly ladies in period costumes, fixing their hair. Startled, she went to get help, but they were gone.

AT YOUR SERVICE. Some ghost stories are just classier than others. Even better, when they take place in one of Michigan's most beautiful estates—the 31,000-square-foot Fairlane Manor in Dearborn. Henry Ford named Fairlane after his grandfather's home in Ireland. It was the last home he and his wife, Clara, lived in before his death in 1947. Construction started in 1914 and included unusual touches such as a bowling alley, an indoor pool, and a skating house. Also on the grounds: 500 birdhouses. The property has been well-maintained with a little help from Clara's favorite maid, who has been seen wandering the halls with towels, and Henry's butler, who has been known to clean up after messy visitors. He has also been seen carrying a drink.

Skeleton Crew. Guides have heard people splashing in the pool, which is especially odd since it has long been filled in with concrete. Henry also built a powerhouse, with a tunnel to connect it to the main house, and that is where guides have heard footsteps at odd times. Some think it is Henry himself, who walked this tunnel most nights after dinner to his powerhouse workshop. In the large garage, a ghostly chauffeur has even been sighted, faithfully polishing one of Ford's finest cars or sitting behind the wheel. No matter if one sees a member of Ford's ex-staff or not, the beautiful house and grounds alone are worth exploring. These have to be some of the world's proudest ghosts.

Ten

THE DETROIT HOUDINI TRAIL

FINAL PERFORMANCE. The famous magician and escape artist Harry Houdini (also known as Ehrich Weiss) made many visits to Detroit. Sadly, that is where he died in 1926, but his connections to the city still remain. Some of his most famous stunts were performed here. (Courtesy of the Library of Congress.)

ESCAPE, DETROIT-STYLE. In November 1906, Houdini, with bound legs and hands, jumped off the Belle Isle Bridge into the cold Detroit River, which was later reported as being frozen solid. He also escaped a Detroit jail cell a year earlier and a locked 75-gallon can of Detroit Creamery milk in 1911 (left). In October 1922, he was suspended upside-down in a straitjacket from the top of the Fyfe Building (below). He also made appearances at the Majestic Theater on Woodward Avenue, which opened in 1915 and is still a top performance venue (with a 106-year-old bowling alley). "Papa" Joe Zainea's family has owned the Majestic since 1946 and restored the façade and marquee to its Art Deco beauty (facing page, above). Staff have seen ghostly figures wandering after hours. Houdini's last performance was at the nearby Garrick Theater, which no longer exists. (Both, courtesy of the Library of Congress.)

GIVING UP THE GHOST. Although Houdini had a fever of 104 degrees, he still took the stage and performed his "Three Shows in One" (the three acts were Magic, Escapes, and Exposure of Fraudulent Mediums) at the Garrick Theater in Detroit on October 24, 1926. Houdini had received an unexpected stomach punch a few days earlier in Montreal and had not been feeling well. He was finally persuaded to leave the Statler Hotel, where he was staying, and go to Detroit's Grace Hospital (below). Doctors diagnosed him with peritonitis, and he died a week later on October 31. His last words were, "I'm tired of fighting." His body was then stored and embalmed at the Hamilton Funeral Home on Cass Avenue (next page, above). This building later became a music school, where a receptionist claimed to see Houdini's ghost several times.

STILL WAITING FOR AN ENCORE. Houdini was planning a new stunt called "Buried Alive"— surviving for a long period of time in a bronze casket, displayed in theater lobbies for publicity. In a twist of fate, that casket was used to send his body back to New York City for burial. Some magicians and fans still come to Detroit to try to contact Houdini, although he famously enjoyed debunking the spiritualists that were so popular during that time. Yet, after Houdini died, his wife, Bess, would come to Detroit to try to contact him through séances held at Detroit's Masonic Temple. She waited to hear their secret phrase "Rosabelle, Believe," an old vaudeville song they loved. Bess gave up after a decade and said, "Ten years is enough to wait for any man." But one can still hope he will appear.

BIBLIOGRAPHY

99wfmk.com

Gilbert, Helen Frances. *Tonquish Tales*. Plymouth, MI: Pilgrim Heritage Press, 1984.

———. *Tonquish Tales Volume 2*. Plymouth, MI: Pilgrim Heritage Press, 1984.

Godfrey, Linda S., *Mark Sceurman, and Mark Moran. Weird Michigan: Your Travel Guide to Michigan's Local Legends and Best Kept Secrets*. New York: Sterling Publishing, 2006.

Hauck, Dennis William. *Haunted Places: The National Directory*. London: Penguin, 1997.

historicdetroit.org

Hunter, Gerald S. *Haunted Michigan: Recent Encounters with Active Spirits*. Holt, MI: Thunder Bay, 2000.

———. *Haunted Michigan 3: The Haunting Continues*. Holt, MI: Thunder Bay, 2013.

Hunter, Gerald S. *More Haunted Michigan: New Encounters with Ghosts of the Great Lakes State*. Holt, MI: Thunder Bay Press, 2005.

lostinmichigan.net

michigansotherside.com

motorcityghosthunters.com

oldshipbuilder.com

Parker, Virginia Bailey. *Ghost Stories and Other Tales from Canton*. Canton, MI: Canton Historical Society, 1998.

Oleszewski, Wes, and Wayne S. Sapulski. *Great Lakes Lighthouses, American & Canadian: A Comprehensive Directory/Guide to Great Lakes Lighthouses, American & Canadian*. Gwinn, MI: Avery Color Studios, 2011.

passionforthepast.blogspot.com

portalparanormalsociety.com

semghs.org

Uptergrove, Mimi. *Ann Arbor Area Ghosts*. Atglen, PA: Schiffer Pub., 2008.

ghosthighway.wordpress.com

wildabouthoudini.com

INDEX

DISCOVER THOUSANDS OF LOCAL HISTORY BOOKS FEATURING MILLIONS OF VINTAGE IMAGES

Arcadia Publishing, the leading local history publisher in the United States, is committed to making history accessible and meaningful through publishing books that celebrate and preserve the heritage of America's people and places.

Find more books like this at
www.arcadiapublishing.com

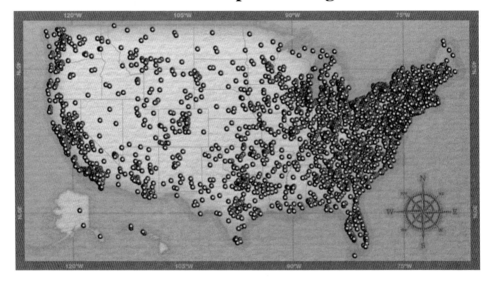

Search for your hometown history, your old stomping grounds, and even your favorite sports team.